The Beast System

THE BEAST SYSTEM

Europe In Prophecy

by
Hilton Sutton

A Study of Revelation

Chapters 13 and 17

HARRISON HOUSE
Tulsa, Oklahoma

Unless otherwise indicated,
all Scripture quotations are taken from
the *King James Version* of the Bible.

Copyright © 1981 by Hilton Sutton
Mission To America
736 Wilson Road
Humble, Texas 77338
ISBN 0-89274-193-7

Published by Harrison House, Inc.
P. O. Box 35035
Tulsa, Oklahoma 74135

Printed in the United States of America

Contents

Introduction

In my many years of preaching and teaching the wonderful victory that is ours through God's beautiful prophetic Word, I've been asked more questions about the Beast than I'd care to count.

Is the Beast a man? Men? A child? A computer?

Is it the apostate church?

Or is it the military-industrial complex?

If you refer to one popular Bible dictionary for a definition of the Beast, you will read that the Beast is: "An Apocalyptic symbol of brute force."

Is that what the Beast is? Just brute force?

God's children are asking these questions because there is a serious lack of accurate and sound teaching in the Church today on Bible prophecy. There is a real need for Bible prophecy teaching that is true to God's Word, yet presented in terms simple enough that we can understand them. God's beautiful prophetic Word makes up approximately one third of His Book, and He never intended for us to ignore it, or to be confused or intimidated by it.

That's why I've written this book: to give you the Holy Spirit's definition of the Beast, to tell when it will be revealed and what its effects will be on the world.

I've used biblical facts and supported them with historical facts to give you a description you can understand of the Beast in the past, the present, and the very near future.

You'll read about Satan's secret plans to take over the entire world, and the Church's devastating impact on these plans — and on the Beast.

Best of all, you'll see that it isn't difficult at all to correctly interpret God's prophetic Word — **if** you are willing to invest a bit of study.

Maranatha!
Hilton Sutton

1
The Beast
and
His System

Just What Is "The Beast"?

There are many conflicting opinions today concerning the Beast of the book of Revelation, and this is not surprising.

Some would have us believe the Beast is nothing more than a gigantic computer. Others tell us the Beast is a plastic financial system, that those credit cards we carry are leading us down the broad pathway to hell.

One major cult identifies the Beast as the Antichrist; then it tells us there are many antichrists all over the world right now, and that you are probably living next door to one of them.

11

At a time like this, with so much confusion around us, let us turn to God's Holy Word for sound instruction. The answer is there for all who will take the time to look for it. In fact, we don't have to look much farther than Revelation, chapters 13 and 17.

Let's begin by clearing up one major point of confusion. In the book of Revelation the Apostle John does use the word *beast* to describe the Antichrist; but he also uses *beast* to describe the Antichrist's assistant, the False Prophet. He uses *beast* again to describe the Antichrist's system — a vast, satanic system of government, commerce, and religion which is being put together today. The European-Mediterranean area is the geographical location in which the pieces are presently being prefabricated.

The System, the Antichrist, the False Prophet — all three are described by John as beasts. As you will soon see, there really wasn't any better word for John to use.

Introducing The System

In the first verse of Revelation, chapter 13, John writes:

And I stood upon the sand of the sea, and saw a beast rise up out of the sea, having seven heads and ten horns, and upon his horns ten crowns, and upon his heads the name of blasphemy.
Revelation 13:1

So the beast rises up out of the sea. Is he some kind of a great fish? Certainly not! In the Bible if the term *sea* is used, but not in reference to a specific body of water, it then refers to masses of people.

This rule of interpretation becomes clear from prayerfully reading Jeremiah 51:55, Isaiah 17:12, Psalm 65:7, Daniel 7:2 as interpreted by

Daniel 7:17, Jude 13, Revelation 17:5, and Revelation 19:6.

The Beast System rises up from the people as they are controlled, manipulated, and brought together by a dynamic leader. This system is indeed satanic. (Notice that upon each head there is a crown; this is explained in Revelation, chapter 17.)

And the beast which I saw was like unto a leopard, and his feet were as the feet of a bear, and his mouth as the mouth of a lion: and the dragon gave him his power, and his seat, and great authority.

Revelation 13:2

The leopard, bear, and lion relate to Daniel, chapter 7. You will soon see how beautifully the prophecies in Daniel correlate with the prophecies in the book of Revelation.

Note that the Beast System gets might, dominion, and authority from the dragon. *Who is the dragon?* He is clearly identified in the book of Revelation, especially chapter 12, as Satan.

2

The Antichrist

And I saw one of his heads as it were wounded to death; and his deadly wound was healed: and all the world wondered after the beast.

And they worshipped the dragon which gave power unto the beast: and they worshipped the beast, saying, Who is like unto the beast? who is able to make war with him?

Revelation 13:3,4

Through verse 4 John has been speaking of the Beast System of seven heads and ten horns, but now he begins to describe the man who heads the Beast System. Note that one of the beast's seven heads was struck a fatal blow that was healed. There will be more about this later.

And they worshipped the dragon which gave power unto the beast: and they worshipped the beast, saying, Who is like unto the beast? who is able to make war with him?

And there was given unto him a mouth speaking great things and blasphemies; and power was given unto him to continue forty and two months.

Revelation 13:4,5

Verse 5 refers directly to the man destined to become the Antichrist — a man who undoubtedly is alive today. But, so long as the Church is still on the earth, this man cannot begin to function as Antichrist. He Who restrains him has not yet been taken out of the way.

"He Who restrains him" is the Holy Spirit-empowered Church. The true identity of "He Who must be taken out of the way" is the Church, not the Holy

Spirit.[1] There can be no other identity that harmonizes with all Scripture.

The Apostle Paul clearly establishes that the Church is the Body of Christ of which Christ is the Head. Therefore, the Church is "He"; and the Church must be taken out of the way, or the "Man of Sin," the Antichrist, could never be revealed.

Notice that three times in 2 Thessalonians 2:1-9 Paul declares that the Antichrist must be revealed, but not until his time.

Daniel, chapter 9, verses 24-27, establishes the fact that Satan is able to negotiate an agreement with many at the beginning of God's final week of work to bring all Israel back to Himself. This agreement is negotiated by the Antichrist.

Therefore, we know exactly when the Antichrist begins his assignment. That assignment cannot begin until the

Church, Who has been withholding Satan's plan for more than 1900 years, has been taken out of the way. (By the way, the final 70th week of God's dealings with Israel is exactly seven years long.)

This man, like his system, will then get his power and authority from Satan. The 42 months (3½ years) of Revelation 13:5 refers to the second half of the Tribulation Period.

During the first half of the Tribulation, the Antichrist is not worshiped as God. He is then operating as a world diplomat, as a skilled world leader who is putting all the pieces of the System together and convincing the nations that he is what they need. The Antichrist wants all the nations on his bandwagon so that when the time is right (at mid-Tribulation), he will be able to assert his authority over all governments and declare himself to be the god of this world.

The Antichrist has great ability as an orator, as we read in Daniel and Revelation:

And he opened his mouth in blasphemy against God, to blaspheme his name, and his tabernacle, and them that dwell in heaven.

Revelation 13:6

Notice that this man has no regard for God whatsoever. At the beginning of his 42-month tour of duty as god of this world, he speaks blasphemy against God, heaven, and everything that is in heaven. In particular, I want you to note that he blasphemes *them that dwell in heaven.*

Why Does He Blaspheme Those In Heaven?

The Antichrist does this in frustration. He is trying to hide his frustration from the world by disguising it with arrogance. But what frustrates him so much?

There has been a group of people growing by leaps and bounds that has been a real thorn in his side. They are the Tribulation saints. Actually, these are two groups of people: the 144,000 young Jewish evangelists from Revelation, chapters 7 and 14, and the Great Multitude of sinners (Rev. 7:9-17) who were saved during the first half of the Tribulation through the anointed and *very* effective ministry of the 144,000.

All this occurs after the Church has been raptured — after you and I have been taken to heaven to be with the Lord forever.

"Now just a minute," you say. "Revelation 7:9-17 shows the Great Multitude in heaven standing before the throne of God. They came *out* of the Tribulation, but you say the Church was raptured *before* the Tribulation began. If the Rapture has already taken place, how does the Great Multitude end up in heaven? And what does all this have to do with the Antichrist being frustrated?"

It is true that the rapture of the Church has already taken place; but where in the Bible does it say that there is only one rapture? There is no such teaching.

Enoch was raptured. (Read Gen. 5:24; Heb. 11:5.)

Elijah was raptured in the presence of Elisha and many other witnesses. In fact, they sent fifty men who searched for Elijah for three days but did not find him. (Read 2 Kings 2:1-18.)

The Lord Jesus was raptured while His disciples were watching. (Luke 24:51; Acts 1:9.)

The Two Witnesses of Revelation, chapter 11, will be raptured. (Read verse 12.) This event will be televised, with the entire world watching via satellite.

In Revelation, chapter 7, we see standing before the throne of God a vast host — a great multitude which no one could number and which had come out of the Great Tribulation.

How did they get there?

How else? The same way the Church got there 3½ years earlier — a rapture. At mid-Tribulation the many converts of the 144,000 who worship not the Antichrist, but Jesus Christ, are taken up to join you and me and the rest of the Church with the Lord. Praise God!

"That's wonderful," you say, "but you still haven't told me why the Antichrist is so frustrated."

The reason is that during this time the Antichrist has been trying to set the stage to declare himself to be God; but at the same time, thousands upon thousands of Jewish Oral Roberts and Billy Grahams have been leading people in droves to their Messiah, the Lord Jesus Christ. The very fact that no one could number the Great Multitude shows that the anointed ministry of the 144,000 was particularly effective.

You can be sure that both the Antichrist and Satan are very frustrated. You can be sure that the Antichrist wants very badly to destroy the 144,000 and their great multitude of converts. But he never succeeds. In fact, throughout the entire Tribulation, the Antichrist never succeeds at all in fully developing Satan's plan. Every time he seems to be having a measure of success, the Lord kicks the props out from under him.

The Antichrist is trying to set things up to declare himself to be God; but before he can do that, he must do something about this Holy Spirit-led revival going on all over the place. So Satan and the Antichrist and all his forces set out to destroy what is God's (the Great Multitude), but God will not allow this. The Great Multitude is simply taken to heaven, where the wrath of Satan and the Man of Sin can never reach them.

Now, the Antichrist has yet another frustrating problem. Approximately 3½ years earlier, the Church was raptured. Millions and millions of people from every land and every walk of life, both those who were dead and those who were alive, rose up into the clouds to meet their Lord in the air. Undoubtedly, this demonstration alone of the Lord's almighty power helped the ministry of the 144,000 a great deal.

Now another host of people has risen up to meet the Lord!

Those remaining on the earth want an explanation for all this, so they turn to their great world leader, the Antichrist. What does he do? He blasphemes *them that dwell in heaven*.

Power Over The Tribulation Saints

And it was given unto him to make war with the saints, and to overcome them: and power was given him over all kindreds, and tongues, and nations.

Revelation 13:7

That sounds bad, doesn't it? Power to overcome the saints in all the nations was given to the Antichrist. But the key to understanding the true meaning of this scripture is given to us in verse 2:

And the beast which I saw was like unto a leopard, and his feet were as the feet of a bear, and his mouth as the mouth of a lion: and the dragon gave him his power, and his seat, and great authority.

Who gave the Antichrist such power and authority? It was *the dragon* — Satan himself.

You should know that the power and authority of Satan cannot even begin to compare with the almighty power and total authority of the Lord God of Hosts. Those who believe that Satan is as powerful as God, or even *almost* as powerful, need to read their Bibles a bit more.

Satan is not even as powerful as a fully armored child of God who uses weapons of war that are not carnal, not intellectual, but mighty through God. (2 Cor. 10:4.) Blow for blow, Satan cannot match a child of God who moves by faith on the authority of the Word of God.

That's why the Apostle James writes, *Resist the devil, and he will flee from you* (James 4:7). The word *resist* is a strong word. It means "to strive or work against, to fight off, to withstand." You can't just say "boo" to the Devil and have him run off.

You need to study the Word and realize all that the Word makes available to you. Read Ephesians

6:10-18 and understand the difference between the child of God, who draws his strength from God's boundless might, and the Man of Sin, who is given the power of an already-defeated enemy.

Note that the dragon gives the Antichrist power over all kindreds and tongues and nations. If this is the case, then all the nations of the world should come under the rule of the Antichrist; but this is not true.

According to the prophet Zechariah, chapter 14, we learn that all nations do not bow down to the Antichrist.

Not all nations take the mark of the Beast described in Revelation, chapter 13.

Not everyone will worship the image of the Beast.

Ten nations from the European area in particular do follow the Antichrist, and toward the end of the Tribulation the Oriental armies assist the Antichrist at the Battle of Armageddon against the Lord Jesus Christ; but other nations of the world will successfully resist the Antichrist.

Egypt is included in that number; and if Egypt can successfully resist the Antichrist, then other nations can and will. Clearly the power and authority that comes from Satan leaves a lot to be desired.

And all[2] that dwell upon the earth shall worship him, whose names are not written in the book of life of the Lamb slain from the foundation of the world.

If any man have an ear, let him hear.

He that leadeth into captivity shall go into captivity: he that killeth with the sword must be killed with the sword. Here is the patience and the faith of the saints.

Revelation 13:8-10

Many people will bow down and worship the Antichrist. Following the scripture that tells us this, we have an admonition for the Tribulation saints, especially those few who will be saved during the second half of the Tribulation, to not use weapons that are carnal or intellectual.

3

The False Prophet

And I beheld another beast coming up out of the earth; and he had two horns like a lamb, and he spake as a dragon.

Revelation 13:11

We began this study with the godless Beast System. Then we covered the Antichrist, also called a beast. Now we read about yet another beast who has the appearance of a lamb, indicating a religious identity; but when he opens his mouth to speak, he speaks like a dragon. We have his number quickly enough! He looks like a lamb but speaks like a dragon — a wolf in sheep's clothing, false religion. Let's keep this fact in mind until we get into chapter 17.

And he exerciseth all the power of the first beast before him, and causeth the earth and them which dwell therein to worship the first beast, whose deadly wound was healed.

Revelation 13:12

This second man, also called a beast, has a main mission: He directs the worship of the people to the Antichrist and exercises the power of the first beast. We've already covered where that power came from.

And he doeth great wonders, so that he maketh fire come down from heaven on the earth in the sight of men,

And deceiveth them that dwell on the earth by the means of those miracles which he had power to do in the sight of the beast; saying to them that dwell on the earth, that they should make an image to the beast, which had

the wound by a sword, and did live.
Revelation 13:13,14

Once more take note of the fact that one of the heads of the seven-headed Beast has been wounded unto death and then restored. The fatal wound was administered with a sword, an implement of military destruction. This will be clarified when we get into chapter 17.

Deception

Both of these "beast-men" are miracle workers — the second in particular. With all the mighty power of the dragon behind the Antichrist and the False Prophet, these miracles really ought to be something. Right? Wrong!

The Apostle Paul tells the church at Thessolonica that these are *lying wonders*. They will appear to be miracles, but they are not. They are only acts of deception. (Read 2 Thess. 2:9-11.)

And deceiveth them that dwell on the earth by the means of those miracles which he had power to do in the sight of the beast; saying to them that dwell on the earth, that they should make an image to the beast, which had the wound by a sword, and did live.

And he had power to give life unto the image of the beast, that the image of the beast should both speak, and cause that as many as would not worship the image of the beast should be killed.

Revelation 13:14,15

Now it has happened: The Antichrist has announced that he is God, that all religion centers around him, and that everyone must worship his image. Those who will not worship the Antichrist and his image are threatened with death.

Those of you who have studied the book of Revelation with me or have listened to my series of cassettes on

Revelation know that at this very time
— when the Antichrist and the False
Prophet are trying to put this system
into effect — God has released His
wrath against Satan. The Antichrist
and the False Prophet really have their
hands full. Try as they might, they just
cannot take over the worship of the
world and everybody on it.

666

*And he causeth all, both small and
great, rich and poor, free and bond, to
receive a mark in their right hand, or in
their foreheads.*

Revelation 13:16

Here we read about "the mark of
the Beast," which is indelibly stamped
on all those who accept the Beast
System and follow the man who heads
it.

*And that no man might buy or sell,
save he that had the mark, or the name
of the beast, or the number of his name.*

Here is wisdom. Let him that hath understanding count the number of the beast: for it is the number of a man; and his number is Six hundred threescore and six.

Revelation 13:17,18

We know that the number of the Beast is 666.

Some folks try to use numerology in an attempt to understand the mark of the Beast. Let me tell you, it just cannot be done. If you look up the definition of numerology in a good dictionary, you will find that it has to do with the *occult* meaning of numbers.

The Apostle Paul didn't tell us to study numerology. He said, "Study the Word." When we do that, we learn that there is an identification mark which involves the number 666 to identify all the people who get involved with that system and follow the Beast. The Lord hasn't given us any more detail.

Therefore, we should be satisfied with the simplicity of the Word of God; then we won't get hung up in all sorts of speculations.

4
Summary of Revelation 13

We are now at the end of Revelation, chapter 13. Let's review what we have learned thus far.

There is a Beast System of seven heads and ten horns, which we will begin to clarify as we move into chapter 17.

We have met two "beast-men."

The first of these heads up the Beast System. In the first 3½ years he appears to be a great orator, diplomat, and world leader able to bring genuine and lasting peace to all the world. Those whose names are not written in the Lamb's Book of Life will believe this, having rejected the Prince of

Peace — the Lord Jesus Christ. They don't know that lasting peace can never come until Jesus Christ returns to this earth and takes over all the governments of the world.

The second "beast-man," the False Prophet, has a religious identity.

These two "beast-men" create an image and a system of worship. Then they decree that everyone must participate in worshiping the Beast (which includes accepting the mark of the Beast), or be put to death.

5
The Harlot

Chapter 17 of Revelation continues our study of the Beast System. This is a very important chapter because it describes the harlot, "the great whore" of the book of Revelation.

This harlot has been around since the beginning of time — she is false religion. She really got under way with the collapse of Israel and during the time of the great Gentile world empires.

And there came one of the seven angels which had the seven vials, and talked with me, saying unto me, Come hither; I will shew unto thee the judgment of the great whore that sitteth upon many waters.

Revelation 17:1

In verse 15 the angel declares that "many waters" represent many people and nations.

With whom the kings of the earth have committed fornication, and the inhabitants of the earth have been made drunk with the wine of her fornication.

Revelation 17:2

This whore has tremendous influence over the peoples of the earth, especially over their leaders; and, indeed, such has always been the way of man. Harlots have always had tremendous influence over leaders and kings, and occasionally this comes to the surface in our news media.

So he carried me away in the spirit into the wilderness: and I saw a woman sit upon a scarlet coloured beast, full of names of blasphemy, having seven heads and ten horns.

Revelation 17:3

Now we see the tie-in with chapter 13 which is where we originally met the Beast with seven heads and ten horns.

But what is the Beast doing? He is carrying the harlot. As you will soon learn, he hates having the harlot on his back. Even so, you can see the close relationship between the System and this great godless religious identity which is actually controlling part of the System.

It should be clear enough by now that the Beast System is threefold, consisting of government, commerce, and religion. (The previous great Gentile empires also consisted of government, commerce, and religion.)

The harlot directly controls the religious third of this satanic trinity. The masses of humanity on earth have always been controlled, not really by government or commerce, but by religion; and those religions have always gained control of government and commerce sooner or later. This is the technique that Satan has used almost from the very beginning to wreck entire countries.

And the woman was arrayed in purple and scarlet colour, and decked with gold and precious stones and pearls, having a golden cup in her hand full of abominations and filthiness of her fornication.

Revelation 17:4

Can the Holy Spirit make it any clearer that this harlot of false religion is filthy — horribly filthy?

A Mystery

And upon her forehead was a name written, MYSTERY . . . .

Revelation 17:5a

This word *mystery* tells a whole story in itself.

All religions outside of Christianity are built on mysteries that are impossible to understand and on fables about mysterious things that never happened nor existed except in the mind of Satan.

The aspect of mystery shared by all false religions of the world is what makes them able to be controlled by witchcraft.

Having spent years in the Orient and in Asia, I found that those who were involved with Buddhism, Hinduism, Islam, and so on, worshiped demons, with plenty of witchcraft included. The same is true for clairvoyants, soothsayers, astrologers, and gurus. First one, then another, comes talking with great flowing words about light, ultimate knowledge, and seeking mind control.

If these demon-inspired religions really worked, then Asia and the Orient ought to be virtual utopias by now since those false religions have been practiced there for thousands and thousands of years. Yet these areas of the world are the most depressed and troubled on the face of the earth, while their false religions with such deep, irrelevant mysteries go on. Amazing, isn't it?

Babylon The Great

And upon her forehead was a name written, MYSTERY, BABYLON THE GREAT, THE MOTHER OF HARLOTS AND ABOMINATIONS OF THE EARTH.

Revelation 17:5

The harlot's second title, *Babylon The Great*, gives us a good deal of insight. Because of the name *Babylon*, we immediately see the tie-in with the Beast System. As you will soon learn, the Beast System began with the early Babylonian Empire, an empire controlled by witchcraft. This was the first Gentile empire that the harlot used for her anti-God activities.

But let's not forget the latter Babylonian Empire, otherwise known as BABYLON THE GREAT.

"Why?" you ask. "Is there something special about that Babylonian Empire?"

There sure is! It was through this empire that the harlot took total control over God's chosen people. She used this empire to take Judah and Jerusalem into captivity in 606 B.C. (Thus began the "times of the Gentiles" which the Lord Jesus spoke of in Luke 21:24.)

Another very important point about the latter Babylonian Empire is that with this empire Daniel picked up his astounding end-time prophecy beginning in Daniel, chapter 2.

In 606 B.C., King Nebuchadnezzar's armed hordes beseiged and captured

Jerusalem. They carried Daniel back to Babylon, along with Shadrach, Meshach, Abednego, and many others. Then the king had a prophetic dream which deeply troubled him. All of his witches, sorcerers, magicians, and astrologers were unable to interpret it; but after Daniel prayed, God gave him the dream and the interpretation.

The dream was of a mighty and terrifying image — the statue of a man. His head was of gold, his breast and arms of silver, his belly and thighs of bronze, his legs of iron, and his feet of iron and clay.

Daniel says to Nebuchadnezzar, king of Babylon, "You are the head of gold." (Dan. 2:38.) This, plus the rest of Daniel's interpretation, relates perfectly with Revelation, chapter 17, as you will soon see.

Mother of Harlots and Abominations

Getting back to the harlot, the Holy Spirit calls her the "mother of harlots."

This is not merely a reference to prostitution of the human body, but to all types of harlotry, filth, and abominations. This is a profound lesson to learn.

We discussed earlier that the systems which control man are threefold, consisting of government, commerce, and religion. Here the Holy Spirit tells us that the mother of harlots and abominations — the origin of all harlotries, filth, atrocities, and abominations of the world — is the great harlot, false religion. Upon her forehead is written the name *Mystery, Babylon The Great.*

And I saw the woman drunken with the blood of the saints, and with the blood of the martyrs of Jesus: and when I saw her, I wondered with great admiration.

And the angel said unto me, Wherefore didst thou marvel? I will tell thee the mystery of the woman, and of the beast that carrieth her, which hath the seven heads and ten horns.

Revelation 17:6,7

This harlot is responsible for the death of the martyrs and saints of Jesus, from the time of her very beginning, up to and into the Tribulation Period.

Seven Mountains

The beast that thou sawest was, and is not; and shall ascend out of the bottomless pit, and go into perdition: and they that dwell on the earth shall wonder, whose names were not written in the book of life from the foundation of the world, when they behold the beast that was, and is not, and yet is.

And here is the mind which hath wisdom. The seven heads are seven mountains, on which the woman sitteth.

And there are seven kings . . . .

Revelation 17:8-10

This scripture needs to be closely examined. For many years people have read this and jumped to the conclusion that these seven mountains are seven hills and that they have to be the seven hills of Rome, Italy. Therefore, the harlot must be the Roman Catholic church.

Nothing could be further from the truth! First of all, Rome is only one of many cities with seven hills. In addition, it is illogical to pick on the Roman Catholic church while ignoring the other religious orders of the earth.

The fact is that all of the manmade religious orders of this world are headed into one massive religious system, and that system — the one great (and godless) world religion — comes under the direct control of the harlot described in Revelation, chapter 17, during the Tribulation Period.

The merging of major religions that you see going on today is but a forerunner of the one-world religion that makes up a third part of the vast Beast System of government, commerce, and religion.

No one can identify one particular church as the harlot of the book of Revelation. I can't and you can't. This becomes very clear as we examine the Scriptures further.

The Harlot's Seat

As we read in Revelation 17:9, the harlot sits upon seven mountains.

In verse 1 of that chapter, the angel describes her as sitting upon *many waters*. Then in verse 15 he states that *many waters* represent many peoples and nations.

In verse 3 the Apostle John sees her sitting upon the seven-headed Beast.

What does all this mean?

The harlot sits upon seven mountains. Since there are seven kings, it must be that each mountain has a king over it.

The seven mountains correspond with the seven heads of the Beast.[3] But there is a special rule of interpretation for the word *mountain*. If this word is used in Scripture, but not with a reference to a specific mountain, then interpret it to mean "kingdom." Seven kingdoms would certainly have seven kings and correspond with the *many waters* (many peoples and nations) of Revelation 17:1.

This is supported in verse 10 where the angel describes the seven kings:

And there are seven kings: five are fallen, and one is, and the other is not yet come; and when he cometh, he must continue a short space.

Revelation 17:10

Over each one of those mountains, or kingdoms, there is a king. Five of the seven have already fallen; one still exists; and one is yet to come.

These mountains are kingdoms, not the hills of Rome. Therefore, it is not possible that the Holy Spirit was speaking of the Roman Catholic church. The harlot sits upon the total Beast System — all seven heads and the many peoples that it encompasses.

6

The Beast's Seventh Head

Of the seven kings and their kingdoms, we have seen that they correspond with the seven heads of the Beast. *Five are fallen, and one is . . . .*

Was there a kingdom in existence when John wrote this prophecy? Yes, it was the Roman Empire.

If the Roman Empire was the sixth kingdom — the sixth head of the Beast — what then were the five that had fallen? They were:

1. the Babylonian Empire, the first of the great Gentile empires.

2. the Assyrian Empire which carried the ten northern tribes of Israel into captivity.

3. the latter Babylonian Empire which under Nebuchadnezzar captured Judah and Jerusalem.

4. the Medo-Persian Empire.

5. Greece under Alexander the Great.

These five had fallen; and the sixth, the Roman Empire, was in control of the people at the time that John was receiving this prophecy.

But what about the *seventh* head?

Five are fallen, and one is, and the other is not yet come; and when he cometh, he must continue a short space.

This seventh head is being put together in Europe and the Mediterranean area today. The seventh head is not a revived Roman Empire. The sixth head was the Roman Empire. The seventh head is another; but it is another head of the same Beast.

The seventh head comes from a revival of the system that produced the Roman Empire — that godless beast system of government, commerce, and religion. In other words, the same system that produced the Roman Empire is coming alive today to produce the Antichrist's empire in the same geographical location — Europe.

Does Daniel Agree?

He most certainly does!

As we have already discussed from Daniel, chapter 2, King Nebuchadnezzar dreamed of a terrifying image which Daniel interpreted. The image had a head of gold — which was King Nebuchadnezzar (Dan. 2:38) — breast and arms of silver, belly and thighs of bronze, legs of iron, and feet of iron and clay.

If the head of this image is King Nebuchadnezzar, then the head corresponds to the third head of the Beast — the latter Babylonian Empire.

The breast and arms of silver are the fourth head of the Beast — the Medo-Persian Empire.

The belly and thighs of bronze correspond to the fifth head — Greece under Alexander the Great.

The legs of iron are the sixth head of the Beast — the Roman Empire.

The two legs represent the divided Roman Empire in A.D. 395: the eastern empire under Constantinople and the western empire which is under Rome.

The ten toes are ten subdivisions.

Isn't it astounding how Daniel's prophecy meshes perfectly with John's? Just another of many infallible proofs that our Book was really written by one Author.

What Will The Seventh Head Be Like?

The seventh head will be a culmination of all that was from the first six heads. Let's go back for a moment to the harlot — false religion.

The first of the great Gentile empires she used was the Babylonian Empire, the first head of the Beast. The harlot — the origin of all filthiness and witchcraft — controlled Babylon through the Beast System. She did this by controlling the people through religion — a third of their system of government, commerce, and religion.

This is how the Beast System got its start.

Looking at the first six heads — these six major Gentile empires of the past — each one simply swallowed up the last one; yet the only thing that really changed was government. Commerce and religion remained the same.

The Babylonian Empire was succeeded by the Assyrian Empire, which was swallowed up by the latter

Babylonian Empire. That empire was
taken over by the Medes and the
Persians. They were defeated by the
mighty Greek Empire, which was
swallowed up by the Roman Empire.

Each succeeding empire just took in
the preceding one, embraced
everything it was, and then added to it.
The harlot, the mother of abominations,
was always there sitting *upon many
waters*, controlling each empire
through its religious third.

If each of these six Gentile empires
swallowed up the last one, yet changed
only government, then think of what it
must have been like when the Apostle
John had been banished to the Isle of
Patmos and was receiving this
prophecy.

The Roman Empire was in power,
and it represented the total wickedness
of all those empires put together.
Witchcraft and astrology flourished.

Religion was predominantly idol worship and entirely demonic. Godlessness was everywhere.

The Beast System continued its rule through the Roman Empire, and the harlot sat on the Beast, exerting her control through her false religious influence.

The seventh head will be worse yet. Think of it! Empowered by Satan, the seventh head will produce the Great Empire of the Antichrist; and the Empire of the Antichrist will give rise to the Antichrist himself and his False Prophet.

The seventh head, the Antichrist's empire, is being prefabricated today. The signs are there for all to see, and we will mention them shortly.

Is the harlot still around? She sure is! In Revelation 17:3 she sits upon the seven-headed Beast. In verse 9 she sits upon seven mountains.

7
Fatal Wound
To The Beast

And I saw one of his heads as it were wounded to death; and his deadly wound was healed . . . .

Revelation 13:13a

. . . to worship the first beast, whose deadly wound was healed.

Revelation 13:12b

. . . that they should make an image to the beast, which had the wound by a sword, and did live.

Revelation 13:14b

Let's consider the nature of this wound.

The *King James Version*, from which we have been quoting, calls it a *deadly wound*. (vv. 3,12.)

The *Revised Standard Version* translates it *mortal wound,* as does the *Modern Language Bible.*

The *Living Bible* calls it a *fatal wound* in verse 3 and a *death wound* in verse 12.

Get the message?

A man, even if he is the Antichrist, cannot recover on his own from a fatal wound. There's no getting around it. That wound is *deadly, mortal,* and *fatal.* Consider the ultimate end of the Antichrist and his False Prophet:

And the beast was taken, and with him the false prophet that wrought miracles before him, with which he deceived them that had received the mark of the beast, and them that worshipped his image. These both were cast alive into a lake of fire burning with brimstone.

Revelation 19:20

Cast *alive* into the Lake of Fire, but there's more . . .

And the remnant were slain with the sword of him that sat upon the horse . . . .

Revelation 19:21a

In Revelation, chapter 19, the Antichrist and the False Prophet are treated as equally alive, differently from the rest who were slain. But if the Beast had a *fatal* wound, then it must have died.

"Well," you say, "suppose the Antichrist did die, but Satan resurrected him?"

Where in the Bible does it say that Satan has the power to resurrect or create life? There is no such scripture. The Devil cannot raise anyone from the dead. Furthermore, God's Holy Word does not indicate that God resurrected the Antichrist as many godly men have believed.

That leaves us with only one other possibility. If it wasn't a beast-man with a fatal wound, then it must have been the Beast System. (Aahh, now we're cooking with gas!)

The head of the Beast that was wounded unto death in Revelation 13:3 was the sixth head, the Roman Empire. The fatal wound to the sixth head caused the entire Beast System to go out of existence and to be later restored as the seventh head.

The sword mentioned in Revelation 13:14 is a military weapon, an implement of military destruction. We all know that Rome decayed from within until she became weak enough for outsiders to conquer her. That's the pat explanation we all have been given in elementary school, but is that *all* there is to it? Could it be that God had something to do with it?

The Stone That Wrecked The Image

As we follow the rule that we must use the Bible to interpret the Bible, let us turn to the prophet Daniel to see if he can shed any light on the matter.

While describing King Nebuchadnezzar's dream, Daniel said:

"As you looked a Stone was cut out without human hands, which smote the image on its feet that were of iron and clay — the burned clay of the potter — and broke them to pieces.

"Then was the iron, the [burned potter's] clay, the bronze, the silver, and the gold, broken *and* crushed together and became like the chaff of the summer threshing-floors, and the wind carried them away, so that not a trace of them could be found. And the Stone that smote the image became a great mountain or rock and filled the whole earth."

Daniel 2:34,35
Amplified Bible

Wow! A Stone smashed the image, bringing the whole thing down so that not a trace of it could be found.

Where did this Stone smite the image? On its *feet*. That's astounding! The feet which support the whole statue is the Roman Empire, the sixth head of the Beast.

"And the Stone that smote the image became a great mountain *or* rock and filled the whole earth." What kind of a Stone is this?

"Come to Him [then, to that] Living Stone which men tried *and* threw away, but which is chosen [and] precious in God's sight.

"[Come] and as living stones be yourselves built [into] a spiritual house, for a holy (dedicated, consecrated) priesthood, to offer up [those] spiritual sacrifices [that are] acceptable *and* wellpleasing to God through Jesus Christ.

1 Peter 2:4,5
Amplified Bible

So Peter helps us understand Daniel, who in turn helps us understand John's Revelation.

The Stone is Jesus Christ, of course. The Stone "filling the whole earth" refers to the Church. When the incarnate Jesus Christ and His Church came into existence, the Beast System went out of existence. If that's the case, then Jesus Christ and His Church must be stronger than the Beast System.

. . . I will build my church; and the gates of hell shall not prevail against it.
Matthew 16:18b

If this is the case, then it must be true that the Beast System cannot come back into existence as long as the Church remains on the earth. Praise the Lord!

In summary, Daniel did not know the incarnate Jesus Christ, but he was given insight into God's plan: that Jesus Christ would come and establish God's kingdom on the earth. The Stone smote the statue on the feet (the Roman Empire, the sixth head of the Beast), and the statue came tumbling down. The Stone (Christ) built a Church of many stones (1 Pet. 2:5) which filled the whole earth.

An Old Testament Type of the Stone

In Judges, chapters 13 through 16, Samson was appointed by God to begin Israel's deliverance from the Philistines before he was born. God endowed Samson with super-human strength; and as long as he was in God's will, his exploits were amazing.

In his death, Samson brought about the collapse and total destruction of the temple of the false god of the Philistines. This god named Dagon was in reality a demon, we conclude from 1 Corinthians 10:20.

According to Judges 16:26,29 the temple (house) of Dagon was supported by two stone pillars, just as Daniel's image was supported by two feet and legs. The temple of Dagon typifies the Beast System, just as does Daniel's image and John's seven-headed Beast. Even though the Philistines had bound Samson, blinded him, and caused his death, Samson destroyed the temple by destroying the two pillars which supported it, just as the Stone smote Daniel's statue on the feet.

Samson slew more of the enemy at his death than he ever slew when he was alive. Therefore, even in his death Samson was God's implement of destruction of the heathen House of Dagon.

Does History Bear This Out?

Judge for yourself! After Christ was crucified, Roman emperor after Roman emperor persecuted the Christians.

Many believe that Nero (A.D. 54-68) executed Paul.

Vespasian (A.D. 69-79) dispatched General Titus to destroy Jerusalem.

After that, Domitian, Hadrian, Antoninus Pius, and Marcus Aurelius all persecuted the Church. Yet Tertullian (A.D. 160-220), who was known as the father of Latin Christianity, wrote the following:

"We are of yesterday. Yet we have filled your Empire, your Cities, your Towns, your Islands, your Tribes, your Camps, Castles, Palaces, Assemblies, and Senate."

Then came the terrible times known in history as the Time of Imperial Persecutions. When that time ended in A.D. 313, approximately one half of the population of the Roman Empire was Christian.

Emperor Constantine (A.D. 306-337) was himself a born-again believer. His "Edict of Toleration" (A.D. 313) granted to all the liberty of following the religion of his choice and was the first edict of its kind in history. He appointed

Christians to public office, exempted ministers from taxes and military service, and assisted in building churches. Slavery, public contests using gladiators, the killing of undesired children, and crucifixion as a means of execution were all outlawed.

Later, the Roman Empire was divided. The western empire, which had its governmental seat in Rome, fell to the Barbarians (Goths, Vandals, and Huns) in A.D. 476.

**Satan's Attempts
To Resurrect The System**

Many times Satan has tried to bring the Beast System back, but he has been unable to do it as long as the Church remains on the earth.

In A.D. 800, Charlemagne attempted to revive the Beast System. His so-called "Roman Empire" included what is today Holland, Belgium, Germany,

France, and Italy. Genghis Khan, Napoleon, Bismarck, Hitler — they all tried, but they all failed.

This proves something — that the Church is more powerful than all of these satanic systems. They all failed, but the Church grows stronger and stronger every day. Praise the Lord!

Again, I point out Jesus' words in Matthew 16:18: *I will build my church; and the gates of hell shall not prevail against it.*

Only when the Church is taken out of the world will Satan be able to bring the Beast System back into existence. Only then will the Antichrist be revealed — not before.

8

Worshiping The System

"Just a minute," you say. "So the Roman Empire was struck a fatal blow and did go out of existence. Revelation, chapter 13, tells me that the people living on earth during the Tribulation will worship the Beast whose deadly wound was healed. It says they'll make an image to the Beast and worship the image. Men don't make idols of systems; they make them of persons. Who would worship a system?"

That's a good question. Born-again believers often have a hard time understanding why anyone would worship a system. But it goes on all the time.

For example: How many people do you know who have made money their idol? Do these people actually worship money? No, they worship the financial *system*. They spend all their energies on figuring new angles to use *the system* to make more money for them. They study *the system*. They live, eat, and breath for *the system*. They think about it by day and dream about it by night. They worship *the system*.

Those who are here during the Tribulation will have been promised great benefits by a persuasive orator who appears to be a man of peace. In addition, the Antichrist will enjoy a limited measure of success during the first half of the Tribulation. Many of these people will want to believe what the Antichrist tells them. They will willingly allow themselves to be deceived.

But people will worship the Antichrist. At mid-Tribulation he will declare himself to be God and be constantly promoted by the False

Prophet. These two men will use every trick to direct the worship of the people away from the system and toward the Antichrist. The Antichrist will be striving to gain total control of the Beast System of government, commerce, and religion.

The Antichrist has control of the government of the seventh head from the beginning of the Tribulation. We learned that he gains control over commerce in Revelation 13:17,18 which told us that no one could buy or sell without the mark of the Beast. But he does not have control over the religious third. The harlot controls the religious third, and through this direct control of the religious third, she exerts indirect control over the entire System.

When the Antichrist declares himself to be God, he will be introducing a new religion. Any existing religious order would have to oppose him. Therefore, if the Antichrist wishes to take total control over the religious third of the System, he will have to do something about the harlot. He will have to find a way to take control away from her. As you will see, the Antichrist will line up no less than ten henchmen to help him do this.

Introducing The Ten Horns

Notice that the seven-headed Beast has ten horns, which corresponds with the ten toes of Daniel's image. The Stone smote the image on its feet. If Satan is to rebuild the image, he will have to start in the same place — the feet, the foundation of the whole Beast System. The ten horns are clearly a part of the seventh head, as shown in Revelation 17:12-17.

The feet of Daniel's image are of iron and clay. The ten toes show ten subdivisions — ten nations. The iron and clay show that some will be as strong as iron, others as weak as clay.

They will try to strengthen themselves by forming alliances with each other, but this will not work because iron and clay do not mix.

Where Are We Today?

It's exciting today for us as God's children to watch prophecy after prophecy being fulfilled. The seventh head of the Beast, the Antichrist's empire, is being put together today. It will consist of government, commerce, and religion, just as all the preceding heads did.

We have a forerunner of world government in the United Nations. The U.N. has already demonstrated more than enough anti-Israeli bias to make Satan proud of it.

We also have a forerunner of the ten-nation confederation in the European Economic Community (E.E.C.) or, as it is more commonly called, the Common Market. Today the E.E.C. has nine nations including England, Ireland, Holland, Belgium, Luxembourg, West Germany, France, Denmark, and Italy. There is one more to go. The Common Market is the present system to keep your eye upon.

So much for governments — what about commerce and religion? The nations of the world and the World Bank have been working feverishly to build a central form of commerce and a single monetary exchange. In the World Council of Churches (W.C.C.), we see a perfectly obvious merging of religious orders, proceeding at a rapid pace.

Should we conclude that the W.C.C. is the harlot? "After all," you say, "it does seem to be moving in that direction."

Yes, it does, but it is not there yet. There are many born-again Christians working inside the W.C.C. for good.

After the rapture of the Church, it will be another matter entirely. After the rapture of the Church, the W.C.C. will be in serious trouble, as you will soon see.

How Long Does The Seventh Head Last?

. . . five are fallen, and one is, and the other is not yet come; and when he cometh, he must continue a short space.
Revelation 17:10

The seventh head lasts "a short space," just long enough for the man who heads it to set up his own operation — with himself as god of the world. This man, the Antichrist, declares himself to be God at mid-Tribulation, and this remains in effect for the remainder of the Tribulation (3½ years).

Before the Antichrist declares himself to be God — when he functions as a great orator and world diplomat and man of peace — he is the leader of the seventh head. His system, the resurrected Beast System, consists of government, commerce, and religion.

After the Antichrist declares himself to be God, he becomes the eighth head. It is one thing to be a great orator and world diplomat. It is quite another thing to be the false god of the world.

And the beast that was, and is not, even he is the eighth, and is of the seven, and goeth into perdition.

Revelation 17:11

Perdition. This word is used eight times in the New Testament. Each time it refers to the final state of the wicked. We have already covered Revelation 19:20, where we see the Antichrist and the False Prophet being cast alive into the Lake of Fire. The Antichrist, then, is the eighth ruler who sets up his kingdom out of the seventh, which is made up of the Common Market nations.

Ten National Leaders

And the ten horns which thou sawest are ten kings, which have received no kingdom as yet; but receive power as kings one hour with the beast.

Revelation 17:12

Here we have ten national leaders, persons known in the world, who pledge their allegiance, power, support, and armies to the man who is leading the System. In exchange for their pledge, he offers them kingdoms when he comes into his full power in the second half of the Tribulation.

These have one mind, and shall give their power and strength unto the beast. These shall make war with the Lamb . . . .

Revelation 17:13,14a

These ten national leaders have one mind; they are completely in support of the Antichrist and all that he stands for, even to the extent of leading their armies against the Lord Jesus Christ at the Battle of Armageddon.

. . . and the Lamb shall overcome them: for he is Lord of lords, and King of kings: and they that are with him are called, and chosen, and faithful.
>   *Revelation 17:14b*

Who are these who are with the King of Kings? Who are *the called, the chosen, and the faithful?*

The Church! Those are the words the New Testament uses to describe the Church that is in heaven, returning with Christ at the end of the Tribulation! The Church is not on earth during the Tribulation. The Church is in heaven during the Tribulation! Praise the Lord!

And he saith unto me, The waters which thou sawest, where the whore sitteth, are peoples, and multitudes, and nations, and tongues.

And the ten horns which thou
sawest upon the beast, these shall hate
the whore . . . .

Revelation 17:15,16a

Why do these ten world leaders
hate "the whore"? Because she
controls the people through false
religion and has indirect power over
them. As soon as the time is right, these
ten leaders will move against her.

. . . these shall hate the whore, and
shall make her desolate and naked, and
shall eat her flesh, and burn her with
fire.

For God hath put in their hearts to
fulfil his will, and to agree, and give
their kingdom unto the beast, until the
words of God shall be fulfilled.

And the woman which thou sawest
is that great city, which reigneth over
the kings of the earth.

Revelation 17:16-18

What a terrible time this will be when the armies of the ten kings are released and in only one hour destroy the harlot and all her trappings. It would certainly have to be with thermonuclear power that this false religious setup (including its headquarter city) is destroyed.

Finally, the stage is set for the Antichrist to do what he has always wanted to do.

Moving Into The Temple

At mid-Tribulation the Antichrist breaks his own peace agreement with Israel and invades the Holy Land. He enters a new temple in Jerusalem (which has been built on the wrong location) and declares himself to be God.

He now has control of government, commerce, and religion. He is now the eighth head. It is now time to try to bring the whole world under the control of his System. It is now time to attempt to seduce the whole world into worshiping him and taking his mark.

This is precisely what Satan wants — that the whole world accept the mark of the Beast. Why? Because there is no salvation for those who take the mark. They have sealed their doom. If the Antichrist can succeed with his plan, then Satan will have finally accomplished what he has always wanted.

Satan will have taken over the whole world. However, a simple study of Revelation, chapter 13, verse 2, reveals that the Antichrist is not on an assignment from God, but from Satan. That assignment is spelled out in verse 7:

It was given unto him to make war with the saints, and to overcome them: and power was given him over all kindreds and tongues, and nations.

Of course, we know that every believer has authority over Satan through the name of Jesus.

Satan has long been trying to find some man to do what he can't do. His track record is that of a loser and his plan is doomed to utter failure.

A careful study of the book of Revelation will reveal that the Antichrist can't make war against the saints, since they will be in heaven. His success over nations is very limited. He will have no more than ten nations supporting him at the time of Armageddon.

The Antichrist will succeed in getting groups of followers in all nations, just as there are communist parties worldwide; but remember, the Antichrist never rules the world.

Greece Becomes The 10th Member

For the first time since its creation in 1957, the Common Market has reached the number of nations needed to create the seventh head of the Beast System.

In 1957 there were only six nations in the organization: France, Italy, West Germany, Luxembourg, Holland, and Belgium.

In 1972 three others — England, Ireland, and Denmark — were added to bring the number to nine.

The year 1979 saw the approval of the application of Greece to become the tenth member. The Greek membership became effective at 12:01 a.m. on January 1, 1981. The Common Market finally became the ten-nation federation[4] predicted by both Daniel and the book of Revelation.

The sixth and last head of this System was the Roman Empire. As Daniel prophesied in chapter 2, the Roman Empire would have two divisions: east and west.

The eastern division, headquartered in Rome, was the real seat of power for the entire Empire. The European Economic Community, or Common Market as it is better known, exists in the same general geographical area as the eastern division of the Roman Empire.

The Middle East makes up the area which was once the western division of the Roman Empire.

Although the Common Market is now a total of ten nations, it will not become the seventh head of the Beast System until someone is selected by the ten heads of state to lead the organization.

This man, whoever he may be, will have the immense task of coordinating the governments, commercial systems, and religions into one harmonious operation — a very difficult assignment.

By the middle of the seven-year period generally called "the Tribulation," he will have succeeded sufficiently to begin his personal attempt to gain control of the entire world — and as the book of Revelation reveals, ho fails!

9
The Antichrist
and
Armageddon

It is now reasonable to assume that the man destined to be the Antichrist is alive today. Many speculate about his nationality, but this is of little importance. We know his base of operation will be in Europe.

The prophet Daniel gives us insight into the nature, ability, and resources of this man. From Daniel 7:8 we learn that the Antichrist will be an outstanding orator.

Chapter 8, verse 23, reveals he will be *a king of fierce countenance* (or magnetic personality), *and understanding dark sentences*. That he will *understand dark sentences* implies he will be a spiritualist of the highest order. The Apostle Paul confirms that he is a medium in 2 Thessalonians 2:9.

In Daniel 8:24 we discover more about the Antichrist. He will be a destroyer and will have so deceived the people that they will applaud his destructive ways. The same verse tells us he will prosper.

The next verse (v. 25) reveals that the Antichrist's policies will cause many crafts to prosper. This will put him in a position to carry on his evil assignment, even against some of the holy people. Remember that Revelation, chapter 6, reveals the opening of the fifth seal, introducing the fact that some Christians of that period will suffer martyrdom at his hands. These martyrs will include the Two Witnesses of Revelation 11:1-12.

Daniel 11:37 declares of the Antichrist: *Neither shall he regard the*

God of his fathers . . . . This has caused
many to believe he will be of Jewish
descent. I want to add that he could be
an apostate Christian.

This same verse reveals that he is
likely to be a homosexual since he has
no desire for women.

His one goal will be to establish
himself as God. (See Dan. 12:37,38; 2
Thess. 2:4.) The Apostle Paul teaches
us that Jesus will destroy the Antichrist
at His glorious return. (2 Thess. 2:8.)
Detailed confirmation of this event is
found in Revelation 19:20.

Identifying The Antichrist

Numerous attempts have been
made by Christian teachers and
theologians to identify the Antichrist.
Up to this date, all have been mistaken.

I can well remember the attempt by
evangelical fundamentalists to make
either Benito Mussolini or Adolph

Hitler the Antichrist. In fact, the fundamentalist camp was almost equally divided between the two candidates. As you well know, both camps lost their chosen Antichrist.

Since that time, the following men have been named as the Antichrist by some segment of the Christian community: Franklin Delano Roosevelt, John F. Kennedy, Henry Kissinger, and King Juan Carlos of Spain.

Someone recently added the name of Ronald Wilson Reagan. President Reagan became a possible candidate strictly on the basis that his three names all had six letter in them, thus 666. This is about the dumbest, most ridiculous thing I have ever heard!

Some Christians are notorious at running off half-cocked with their brain out of gear. Be cautious of Christian "Chicken Littles," who are always sure they have made the discovery of the century about some mystery of God.

The Scriptures clearly teach us that the Antichrist *cannot* be revealed until after the Church is caught up to heaven and it is time for his performance to begin. The reference is 2 Thessalonians, chapter 2, verses 1-9. Three times in this passage of scripture, it is stated that the Antichrist is to be revealed. It is also clear that God controls the time in which he is to be revealed. Therefore, since the Antichrist cannot be revealed until his time, *no one* can possibly identify him.

Please notice that the plan of Satan to bring forth his man is being withheld until "the withholder" is taken out of the way. Only then can the Man of Sin be revealed, not before.

Who Is "The Withholder"?

Some have taught that "the withholder" is the Holy Spirit. However, this cannot possibly be true.

One must remember that the Holy Spirit is "God the Holy Ghost." As God, He is universally present. He is everywhere, all the time. There can be no "taking out" of the Holy Spirit.

The only other possible identity of the "he" of 2 Thessalonians 2:7 which has to be "taken out of the way" is the Church.

Please notice that the Apostle Paul says the "mystery of iniquity" was at work in his time, but was being withheld. Paul is simply saying that, if it were possible, Satan would come forth with his plan involving the Antichrist now; but "the withholder" is present. Paul was speaking of the true Church.

One may reason that the Church is *she* not *he*, but this is a misleading assumption based on the over-emphasizing of the "Bride" aspects of the Church. When one carefully studies the works of the Apostle Paul, the discovery is made that the Church is "the Body of Christ" of which Christ is the Head. Therefore, since Christ is *He*, then the Church — His Body — is *He*.

In Ephesians 4:13 Paul firmly establishes that we believers are coming into the unity of the faith and knowledge of the Son of God, *unto a perfect man*. Therefore, the Church should always be referred to as *He*. Clearly then, the *he* in 2 Thessalonians, chapter 2, that must be taken out of the way before the Antichrist can be revealed is the Church of Jesus Christ.

Moving To Armageddon

And the ten horns which thou sawest are ten kings, which have received no kingdom as yet; but receive power as kings one hour with the beast.

These have one mind, and shall give their power and strength unto the beast.

These shall make war with the Lamb, and the Lamb shall overcome them: for he is Lord of lords and King of kings: and they that are with him are called, and chosen, and faithful.

Revelation 17:12-14

Satan will have tried to take over the whole world, but he's just not going to make it!

The same Stone that struck down the Beast System before and put it out of existence will strike it down again — this time forever and ever!

The same Church whose very presence on the earth made it impossible for the Beast System to exist will return with the Lord to the earth to participate with Him in the millennium.

10

Summary

In this examination of Revelation, chapters 13 and 17, we have studied the Beast with seven heads and ten horns, and we have studied the harlot.

We have learned quite a bit about Satan's plans to bring the whole world under his control; and we have seen that, as always, Satan's plan is imperfect. It does not succeed. It cannot succeed. It was doomed from the start.

We watch with great interest as the seventh head of the Beast System comes together today and nears its completion. We know that the three major parts of the Beast System must be in place to produce the seventh head. We see the governmental part in the making; the commercial part in the making, and the religious part in the making.

All that remains is for some great man to come on the scene who has the ability to put the three prefabricated pieces together. This is the man destined to become the Antichrist, the Man of Sin. But he cannot be released to begin his satanic work until that which restrains him — the Church, the dwelling place of the Holy Spirit — is taken up out of the way. (Read the second chapter of 2 Thessalonians.) Then he begins his program of leadership of the great ten-nation alliance in the European and Mediterranean areas.

Watch these things very closely as they race toward the Great Tribulation because they all testify to one great fact — that Jesus Christ is coming soon! The sound of the trumpet of God is not far off.

Watch as Satan continues to maneuver, and as God continues to outmaneuver him. Watch as the Church is brought more and more into a victorious, commanding position before being caught up to meet the Lord Jesus Christ.

May God bless you real good, and may His wonderful Word become more meaningful and real to you with every passing day!

Maranatha!
Hilton Sutton

Notes

1. What does it mean that the Holy Spirit will be taken out of the world with us? Does it mean that nobody can be saved after the Church is raptured? No, not at all! Remember that the Holy Spirit is God! As God, He has all the power and prerogatives of God.

   For example, He has resurrection power. (Rom. 8:11.) At the time of the rapture of the Church, it is the Holy Spirit Who accomplishes the resurrection of the dead in Christ. Until this time, the earthbound Church has been under the direct supervision of the Holy Spirit; but now, the Church has finished Her assignment, so the Holy Spirit escorts Her to meet Christ and return with Him to the Throne of God. What joy that will be! Read 1 Thessalonians 4:16-18 and Revelation, chapters 4 and 5.

If the Holy Spirit is God, then like God He is omnipresent — present everywhere at once — and His work goes on wherever He wills.

As a Person, the Holy Spirit has been operating here on the earth since the Jewish feast of Pentecost according to Acts, chapter 2. The work of the Holy Spirit on the earth will continue after the Rapture, just as before. How else could the 144,000 be saved? How else could the Great Multitude be saved? Praise God for the continuing work of His precious Holy Spirit!

2. This scripture says, And all that dwell upon the earth shall worship him. ("Him" refers to the Antichrist.) This makes some people wonder how anyone who lives on the earth then can be saved if they all worship the Antichrist.

The answer to this question is in the same sentence. It is all . . . whose names are not written in the book of life of the Lamb slain from the foundation of the world. The word all is not being used in an all-inclusive sense. It is used to indicate that generally there will be followers of the Antichrist from all over the earth, especially from the

European area. Just as communism is strong in Russia and China, one can find pockets or groups of Communists everywhere.

3. Revelation 12:3 supports this. There the seven-headed dragon is presented to us as a symbolic representation of the totally satanic nature of the Beast System. Each of the dragon's seven heads has a crown, indicating that each of the seven heads is a kingdom.

4. The prophet Daniel causes us to believe that there will be more than ten members in the Common Market.

In chapter 7, Daniel speaks of the Antichrist as the "Little Horn" that plucks up or destroys three of the original horns. Yet when he arrives for the Battle of Armageddon, as described in the book of Revelation, he has ten nations with him. This could account for the fact that Spain and Portugal now have made applications and expect to be admitted to the Common Market by no later than 1985.

This action would bring the number to twelve and leave room for yet one more nation.

Who will it be?

As of this writing, I will not speculate. However, I will go on record to declare it will not be the United States as some are erroneously teaching.

Hilton Sutton is regarded by many as the nation's foremost authority on Bible prophecy as related to current events and world affairs.

As an ordained minister of the Gospel, Rev. Sutton served as pastor for several years before being led out into the evangelistic field. Today he travels throughout the world, teaching and preaching the Word. He takes the words of the most accurate news report ever — the Word of God — and relates it to the news today.

Having spent over twenty years researching and studying the book of Revelation, Hilton Sutton explains Bible prophecy and world affairs to the people in a way that is clear, concise, and easy to understand. He presents his messages on a layman's level and shows the Bible to be the most accurate, up-to-date book ever written.

Hilton Sutton and his wife, JoAnn, make their home in Houston, Texas, where he serves as Chairman of the Board of Mission To America, a Christian organization dedicated to carrying the Gospel of Jesus Christ to the world.

To receive Hilton Sutton's
monthly publication, **UPDATE,**
write:
Mission To America
736 Wilson Road
Humble, Texas 77338